A Cold Day

by Lola M. Schaefer

Consulting Editor: Gail Saunders-Smith, Ph.D.

Consultant: Chris S. Orr, Certified Consulting Meteorologist, American Meteorological Society

Pebble Books

an imprint of Capstone Press
Mankato, Minnesota

Pebble Books are published by Capstone Press
1710 Roe Crest Drive, North Mankato, Minnesota 56003.
www.capstonepub.com

Library of Congress Cataloging-in-Publication Data
Schaefer, Lola M., 1950–
    A cold day/by Lola M. Schaefer.
    p. cm.—(What kind of day is it?)
    Includes bibliographical references and index.
    Summary: Simple text and photographs describe and illustrate a cold day, including
what people wear, see, and do.
    ISBN-13: 978-0-7368-0402-8 (hardcover)   ISBN-10: 0-7368-0402-1 (hardcover)
    ISBN-13: 978-0-7368-8620-8 (softcover pbk.)   ISBN-10: 0-7368-8620-6 (softcover pbk.)
    1. Winter—Juvenile literature. 2. Cold—Juvenile literature. 3. Cold weather
clothing—Juvenile literature. [1. Winter. 2. Cold. 3. Cold weather clothing.] I. Title.
II. Series.
QB637.8.S34 2000
551.5′25—dc21   99-19421

Note to Parents and Teachers

The series What Kind of Day Is It? supports national science
standards for units on basic features of the earth. The series also
shows that short-term weather conditions can change daily. This
book describes and illustrates what happens on a cold day. The
photographs support early readers in understanding the text. The
repetition of words and phrases helps early readers learn new
words. This book also introduces early readers to subject-specific
vocabulary words, which are defined in the Words to Know section.
Early readers may need assistance to read some words and to use
the Table of Contents, Words to Know, Read More, Internet Sites,
and Index/Word List sections of the book.

Printed in the United States of America in North Mankato.
042013   007305R

Table of Contents

Today is a cold day.

The temperature is low on a cold day.

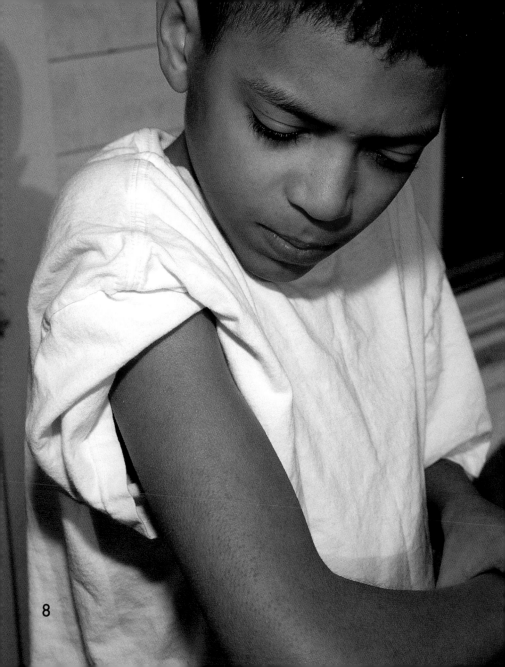

8

You might have
goose bumps
on a cold day.

You might see your breath
on a cold day.

You might see frost on a cold day.

You might see ice
on a cold day.

You might see rain
on a cold day.

You wear warm clothes on a cold day.

You might say, "Brrr,"
on a cold day.

Words to Know

breath—the air you breathe in and out of your lungs; you can see your breath on cold days because it is warmer than the air.

frost—a thin layer of ice crystals that forms on cold surfaces; frost forms outside in freezing weather.

goose bumps—tiny bumps that appear on people's skin when they are cold or frightened

temperature—the measured heat or cold of something; temperature is measured with a thermometer.

Read More

Frost, Helen. *Snow.* Weather. Mankato, Minn: Pebble Books, 2004.

Saunders-Smith, Gail. *Warm Clothes.* Preparing for Winter. Mankato, Minn.: Pebble Books, 1998.

Sipiera, Paul P. and Diane M. *The Seasons.* A True Book. New York: Children's Press, 1998.

Internet Sites

FactHound offers a safe, fun way to find Internet sites related to this book. All of the sites on FactHound have been researched by our staff.
Here's how:

1. Visit *www.facthound.com*.
2. Type in this special code **0736804021** for age-appropriate sites. Or enter a search word related to this book for a more general search.
3. Click on the **Fetch It** button.

FactHound will fetch the best sites for you!

Index/Word List

Word Count: 71
Early-Intervention Level: 8

Editorial Credits

Martha E. H. Rustad, editor; Abby Bradford, Bradfordesign, Inc., cover designer;
  Heidi Schoof, photo researcher

Photo Credits

David F. Clobes, 8, 20
International Stock/Michael Ventura, 6; James Davis, 18
Photo Network/Michael Philip Manheim, 12
Photri-Microstock, 16; Photri-Microstock/Landphoto, 10
Richard Hamilton Smith, 1
Robert McCaw, 14
Shaffer Photography/James L. Shaffer, cover
Unicorn Stock Photos/Andre Jenny, 4